Product of America

Psychological Warfare

Cornelius P. Thomas Jr.

© 2025 by Cornelius Thomas Jr.
Lyrical Giant Media Group

All rights reserved, including the right to reproduce this book or portions thereof in any form whatsoever by author. No part of this book may be reproduced, scanned, or distributed in any print or electronic form without permission. Please do not participate or encourage piracy of copyrighted materials in violation of author's rights.

Library of Congress Cataloging – in Publication Data

Thomas, Jr. Cornelius P.
(Poems, Text)
Sign of the Times Volume 2/ POA
Behind Enemy Lines
ISBN 978-0-578-74006-5

Dedicated to the strength of the oppressed and the resilience to stand in spite of the opposition…

REVELATION 18:1-5, 24

TABLE OF CONTENTS
STAMPED WITH A LABEL

Product of America 2

Blood Line 4

Real Talk 101 6

Rejects and Castaways 8

Family Tree 11

Set Free 14

Labeled 16

The Microwave Process 18

Planted to Grow 20

What is Your Price? 23

Hidden 26

The Intent to Edify 28

The Ink Bleeds 30

Epidemic in the Wilderness 33

At a Stand Still 36

A Constant Struggle 39

Intricate Plots 42

The Story Teller 45

Think Outside of the Box 42

Overthrow Limitations 49

BEHIND ENEMY LINES

Choosing to Be More 53

A Wealth of Knowledge 55

Awake the Sleeping Giant 57

It takes Faith 60

Wisdom is 62

Powerful Pen 64

Follow the Leader 66

Prisoner of Unspoken Words 68

Prophetic Signs 70

Behind Enemy Lines 73

The Remnant 76

Imprisoned by Gravity 78

Thy Will Be Done 81

Exiled 84

Inside 86

What Can I Offer? 88

The Conflict 90

Spiritual Rehabilitation 92

At War with the Devil's Kingdom 95

Beginning of Sorrows Extended 99

STAMPED WITH A LABEL

PRODUCT OF AMERICA
Deuteronomy 28:37, 49, 50, 64-68

America, the Beautiful
My pain or complaint isn't new to you
YAH reveals the hypocrisy
Even though you remove the clues
Confused views
will lead to bad attitudes
PTSD
minds programmed to lose

The 12 tribes have been scattered
seems like we're hustling backwards
Every man is for himself
trying to climb success' ladder
Trying to get to the bag while they're
knocking us off
The family structure infiltrated
the generation is lost

Fatherless, it's hard to get
the youth to embrace patience
We're dodging threats, we started with
nothing when it comes to reparations
Abortion, incarceration, depopulation agenda
We went from Kings and Priests
to "N" words and mimicking Italian mob figures
Monitored, because we're despised
got us thinking that we cannot rise
They took the shackles from our bodies

Cornelius P. Thomas Jr.

placed them on our minds
However we're still here
I'm screaming Qam Yasharahla
Man, we're dying over nothing
there's no value in that dollar

What we're seeing is a *Product of America*
shots are fired in my area
Some say the times are getting scarier
If you pray and watch the signs, you'll be like me
never giving up

Political policies
and biblical prophecies
Are in perfect alignment
we have to flee from idolatry
Get a knee on the neck
shot with hands in the air
Choked, screaming you can't breathe
and still victims of cold stares

Suspicions and stereotypes
division and video likes
Going viral with my last breath
a hashtag for my life

They say that this is my home
but I'm not feeling it
Shouldn't have to protest and march
when I'm supposed to be a citizen

Product of America

BLOOD LINE

Part of the 42nd generation
blood line thorough
The King of kings is my inspiration
it may seem as if I'm solo
But I'm highly protected
by my Rock and Ark of Safety
The righteous stand bold as a lion
it's not wise to underestimate me

A sacrifice among my peers
although some can't even see it
Representing on behalf of nobles
the art of war carries a secret
Inhaling, exhaling
in expectation of the promises
Guaranteed to manifest
so this oppression, I can't stomach it

My descendants are immune
don't know what bondage is
learned to cope with fewer options
Royal blood from on high
has cleansed my impurities and toxins
Not to mention dysfunctional outlooks
refuse to live on my knees
Unless I'm crying out to YAH
true freedom isn't free
*What do I look like begging for equality
when I belong to The Most High?*

Cornelius P. Thomas Jr.

His Kingdom rules over all
I have unseen family ties
Always knew there was more in my blood line
than idolatry, whoredom, and drug addictions
Inferiority complexes and thug living
fit for more than early graves and prison

Greatness came from my lineage that predates
the arrival of slave ships in 1619
Today we're trapped in a mental matrix
spiritually bankrupt and afraid to dream
Last name is Thomas
but that isn't the original truth
Psychological warfare at its finest
the illusion of inclusion is a signature move
From this beast system with no heart
abused in a place called home
This has to be a figment of my imagination
talking about the same issues for so long

Part of the 42nd generation
blood line is supernatural
Christ is my inspiration
never underestimate the radical

Product of America

REAL TALK 101

I come from a section where human life has no value
many have died for less
Drug dealings and senseless killings
call it *the devil's playground*
We're expected to self-destruct and become
suffocated by statistics
There are plenty of single parent homes
many have sacrificed their children to idols
People become dehydrated in the rat race
likened to a hamster on a wheel
…going nowhere fast
Children end up being raised by music videos, sex scenes
from television programs and peer pressure
Why is responsibility such a foreigner?
Demons manifest destruction and corruption through
the unfruitful works of darkness and idolatry
Our only hope is despised and overlooked
Jesus Christ, the Great High Priest
The young men are fascinated by fast money
and thug affiliation
Some never come to the terms that a real man will deny
himself and carry his cross
He will embrace the head position and lead his family
Men and women have switched roles
we address our women by derogatory names
Many females leave the roles of femininity,
lower their standards and settle
Looked upon as a piece of meat
They learn to cope with heartache

suppress emotions and accept defeat
A Poetic Ambassador summoned to speak
so I run it how I get it
I can't just "talk" this righteous talk
I too must live it
We must always lead by example
one's reward will always be determined by one's motive
Dysfunction is a common state
Is this common state of being coincidental?
…or is this the result of a carefully structured plot?
Before I place blame and pass the buck
I'll accept accountability as I look in the mirror
I will say this…
In the spiritual world, there are always hidden hands
operating as puppet masters
There are underlying issues, mental conditions,
demonic suggestion and political oppression as well
The truth will always prevail
whether we stand in favor of it or not
Real talk is needed in delusional times
however many are blind to the plots
They say *United we stand*
but we're divided and that's the plan
The bigger picture is to find purpose in a timely manner
of your life span

REJECTS AND CASTAWAYS

Emotions fall from the pen
landing in between the blue lines of the loose leaf
Transformation takes place
when artistry overtakes the blank sheet
I have acknowledged my foolishness unto YAHUAH
Through Christ, He has given me the keys
to bind and loose
Yet I have been standing outside of the door of delegated
authority knocking
Attempting to revive giants that God
has delivered me from
The old things have passed away
I asked for a closer walk with the Messiah
However emotions shout and pout
at the thought of loneliness
*Shall I continue to surround myself with people who
could care less?*
Demonic spirits do not favor the righteous cause
I've been placed in isolation to receive revelation
A stranger in the earth who desperately awaits
the heavenly homeland
The time is not yet
There is still an assignment to fulfill
a few more giants to kill
Salvation isn't based on how we feel
so we stand strong on the battlefield
In the beginning, the serpent beguiled the woman
who in turn caused man to transgress

Cornelius P. Thomas Jr.

In this season, the enemy is offering demonic suggestion
in the form of females
Agape love is at war with temporary lust
I cannot continue to travel around the same mountains
enough is enough
Verbal homicides and premeditated attempts to destroy
the purpose from heaven
YAHUAH-ELOHIYM has proven to be faithful
since ancient times
Who has been His counselor?
Therefore, I have chosen to trust Him with my all
self-confidence is called arrogance
Now that I don't need man's validation
war has risen against me
I shall continue to press forward
although there's a war in my members
Consumed by wicked imaginations
trapped by the misconception
and threatened by the dark dysfunction
of a lost generation
Stumbling at the same old ideas
yet, old things have passed away
I find myself embracing a mentality that wants to
take me to hell
My spirit knows that I have been chosen
but I have been rejected ever since I could remember
My flesh yearns to be accepted
but I need to kill it with this Word
I represent the underdogs who desire change
they are constantly confronted by trial and error
…evils premeditated

Product of America

Where can we place the blame?
"feels" like I'm going insane
I refuse to stay in this dilemma
because YAH is all-knowing
Christ has already lived all of my tomorrows
He will deliver me from this phase
of being held captive as a mental slave
Blindness finds me in the midst of sunshine
I've tried to fit in and be socially accepted
like a circle among squares
Awkwardly unique
these days originality is rare
Numbered among the rejects
and castaways
Had to suffer pain being the oddball
depression can last for days
…or even longer
…try months, years, or even a lifetime
The Savior was despised and rejected of men
died and rose again to become our Lifeline
It took a lot of inner healing and self- affirmations
to finally get comfortable in my own skin
Fearfully and wonderfully made
the Word of Life can turn boys into grown men
Keeping my mind renewed was the answer
after plucking the traumatic issues up by the root
YAHUAH-Rophe'ka is the *Healer*
the tree is ready to bear good fruit
Emotions fall from the pen
landing in between the blue lines of the loose leaf
Transformation took place, by process He set me free

Cornelius P. Thomas Jr.

FAMILY TREE
Romans 9:1-3

I have a great heaviness and continual sorrow in my heart
For I wish that myself were cursed from Christ for my
brethren, my kinsmen according to the flesh

The elders taught us the street life
thugging and promiscuity
I have come to find that my sexuality
doesn't make me a man
My descendants are trapped in a vicious cycle and
only YAH can save us!
For years and years, we were trained
to live and represent a certain lifestyle
…dysfunctional
Demonic spirits are leading the family
swiftly towards destruction

Today, I am hit with the piercing wounds of truth
there is great error in our ways
Taking YAH'S grace, mercy,
and forgiveness in vain
Mocking Reverend Do Wrong and the scriptures
literally dying to make a name
A reputation
fleeing from purpose
Procrastination
mental sedation and plenty of time wasting

The Light of Christ has shown up at the doorstep of my

Product of America

heart
But to my family, I'm only "Lil Neal"
…the least of the least
Drug addictions, heavy afflictions,
so many contradictions
Thought patterns so out of whack
I constantly seek the Great Physician
The seed of Abraham doesn't necessarily mean
a child of The Most High
I have a great heaviness and continual sorrow in my heart
purpose was predestined

Without doing good or evil, I received an
election from YAH
Trained to love my family, immediate and extended
however the truth brings separation
By no means am I better
this is the same blood line
Grandma cooking in the kitchen
grandpa working hard for a living
No disrespect intended
the family has been hooked on traditional living
superstitions and mental prisons
It is said that the *apple doesn't fall far from the tree*
What was The Most High's intention for bringing my
parents together?
Sick and tired of the broken dreams,
barren expectations and stormy weather
The family tree is fighting to breed
among the most evil of weeds
We all spring from different trees

Cornelius P. Thomas Jr.

expected to bear good fruit
There is beauty and strength in the tree
that continues to grow amidst strange times
Behold the separation at the same time!
The devil persuades to change minds

The strength and resilience of the oppressed
Only God can save us!
I've come to find that my true family is spiritually
connected by the blood of the Lamb
Strangers of the same tribe
part of the universal Body of Christ
Love and determination continues to thrive

The love that I possess for my descendants
produces the sorrow within my heart
Prayerfully, I must keep pressing forward and speak life
on the journey set apart

In memory of James "Lil Mike" Queen

SET FREE
John 8:36

The spell has been broken
once and for all YAH has spoken
Power belongs to the Most High
I am no longer choking
With the cares of this world
indulging in diverse lust
In Jesus there is freedom
to walk in what I trust

Holy Spirit is my guide
counselor and mediator
YAH is a burden bearer
and a pain alleviator
It is good that I've been afflicted
outside it's still storming
Had to endure a long night
but joy will show up in the morning

Take heed to the warnings
this causes demonic attacks to come against me
Evil spirits swarming
doctrines of devils trying to convince me
I once ran with strange children
but my Heavenly Father was overprotective
Never quite understood that constrained feeling
until the Word changed my perspective

Cornelius P. Thomas Jr.

All those years of seclusion
word curses to make me feel worthless
YAH strategically moved the decoys
that came to hinder my purpose
Now self-will is obsolete
all of my needs, He will supply
A grain of wheat must first fall
into the ground and die
To bring forth its fruit
a new season to live
A new reason to live
the blood of Jesus is real

There's a way that seems right to man
death may be at the end of that agenda
There's nothing wrong with knowing
when and where to surrender
I surrender my all
including shortcomings and flaws
A joint-heir with Ha'Mashiach
power and authority to rule, even if I fall
Graced to get back up
endurance wins the race
I can boldly proclaim that I've been set free
the King of glory pled my case
Not guilty is the verdict
thankful for the atonement
Now I can walk like the true king that I am
never mind the opponent

LABELED

Product of America
a fugitive that will contest
Spiritual and economic bondage
desiring the best on this quest
With a cause to protest
the mission isn't geared towards race
Open to unify with all of humanity
those who seek YAH'S face
Military minds
an elite group of frugal men
The Ruach executes through this pen
so listen in

Discipline comes from within
success is a learned behavior
Whether in season or out of season
this soldier's melody can be found on paper
Such ballads are considered intricate
because the Lord's grace is infinite
The vast majority desires more out of life
but don't know how to go from being limited
Some will settle for handouts
while complaining about a hand up
When it comes to ignorance, would rather stand out
when it's time, very few will stand up
and effectively fight for the right things
we have to stop chasing these pipe dreams
We're in a constant war
but overlook strategic set-ups, plots, and schemes

Cornelius P. Thomas Jr.

I take flight from hell fire
to ignite those who are tired
of crumbs from a piece of the pie
…seems like you're living just to die
A fight to get free from manmade labels
when you refuse to bow, you become a rebel
Equal rights shouldn't still be the topic of discussion
Should we just continue to settle?
Nah, that's the wrong answer
I belong to a Higher Power
Labeled as a Kingdom Builder
He doesn't train, shape, and mold cowards

THE MICROWAVE PROCESS

It is a known fact that we have to
go through it to get to it
"Go through what?" one might ask
Trials and tribulations, the learning process,
growing pains…
The things and/ or processes that will help us the most
are usually the very things that we shun
Many times blessings are forfeited by mankind
because they don't show up dressed as blessings
As I dwell in the midst of a confused generation, filled
with information, I've come to find that most of us are
microwave babies
Many of us were raised to flee from hard work
we anxiously seek fulfillment from the here and now
Again, many of us were not raised with silver spoons
but we may have been laced with silver lining
Just because it doesn't feel good to you doesn't
necessarily mean that it's not good for you
To everything in life that is worthwhile,
there is a process that comes with it
The children of YAH must suffer
for righteousness' sake in this world
Christ is our only hope in these strange times
we undergo enormous pressure
But the pressure always leads
to another level of power
Hardships and heartaches
are both found in the development stage
We must go through it to get to it

Cornelius P. Thomas Jr.

"Get to what?" one might ask
The common goal, the promises of God, a level of achievement

Instead of preparing a home cooked meal filled
with substance and nutrients, many would rather
eat on the go
We reach for microwavable junk foods
…quick remedies and easy methods
The path of least resistance
Broad is the way that leads to destruction and many
will choose to travel that path
There is no honor or valor in the easy route
Anyone can go and purchase costume jewelry
however it takes a peculiar customer to invest
in precious jewels
Before one can become wise
they must first play the fool

Many systems and institutions are filled
with microwave babies
Microwavable dishes may vary
yet, they all have one thing in common
…the labels containing directions on how to
obtain the quick fix
I hope you can embrace the metaphors
In an ever changing world, filled with fast paced
environments, none of us can skip the line
or steps needed to achieve greatness
Sometimes, we have to go back to the drawing board
and get back to the basics

PLANTED TO GROW

EL YAHUAH is great and greatly to be praised
He is clothed with honor and majesty
all praises are due to His sovereign name
The Most High instructs His chosen ones
on the paths that were already preordained
At His presence, the earth trembles
the heavens are His throne and the earth
is His footstool
YAH created man for His purpose
Why is it that mankind is so easily sidetracked?
Doctrines of devils lure men from the truth
Some may run and laugh now
but we all must face it later
How could the creation not need the Creator?
In the heavens, all of the inhabitants behold His beauty
they declare His righteousness
He sent His Son to die as a sacrifice and/or kinsman
Redeemer
First, to reconcile the lost sheep of the house of Israel
back unto their ELOHIYM
but the sovereignty of YAH, knowing their rebellion
…that they would reject the Messiah made the free gift
available for all who would believe on Him
Yet, we the people continue to stumble
at YAH'S commandments
If you lend me your ear
I promise to win your heart
These words are not deceptive
but rather Spirit and Life

Cornelius P. Thomas Jr.

We were planted to grow
the growth has been stunted until we get it right
Egypt represents idols and slaves of sin
The poverty-stricken, the oppressor and the oppressed
the house of bondage, lack and so on
the lack of knowledge, the lack of finances, lack of
self-worth, etc…
Victims of the devil's attacks
The wilderness represents the transition, the shaping and
molding process, miracles, and sufficiency
…just enough of YAH'S provision for the journey
The Father is calling for us to be separated
from iniquity and idolatry
The Passover Lamb has been manifested
we are without excuse
The Promised Land represents liberty to praise our
ELOHIYM, EL ELYON… EL SHADDAI
The manifestation of prophecy
living life in peace, prosperity and abundance
The prepared place…
Although the way has been made,
very few will make it to the Promised Land
plagued by fear, doubt, and unbelief
Sidetracked by distractions
many will settle for less
while talking about doing their best
Seeing that history has a way of repeating itself
let us be watchful not to miss our time of visitation
Let us remain prayerful and allow the Spirit of Truth
to lead us
Endurance wins the race

Product of America

and the just shall live by faith
Faith without works is dead
but the way has already been made
I praise the Horn of my salvation
In Him, we find our rest
There is no righteousness apart from Christ
either the seed is corrupted or blessed

Cornelius P. Thomas Jr.

WHAT IS YOUR PRICE?

Do not labor for what you will earn
but rather what you will learn
I know that this is a hard saying
and it raises some concerns
Life has a way of testing us
each human has a needy part of their soul
that becomes vulnerable
If not properly protected…
…it can be bought
Yet, there is another part of the soul that is strong
Once the soul is truly submissive to God
it carries no compromise
Temptations and emotions can cause conflict
or unify and work together
Most people have a price
What is yours?
Emotions can manifest fear
and temptation can manifest greed
Many will disregard direction
preoccupied with trying to speed
Prostitution is not limited to the first thought
that comes to mind
Some people exchange their integrity for a dollar amount
behold the trap in fine print of an unseen contract
The heart becomes involved
the heart is evil above all things
Your heart can expose secrets about you that you never
knew existed
No one is exempt

Product of America

It is the devourer of mankind who persuades humans
to auction off their souls
In search of fame or to look the part
for the spectators
Vanity of vanities
...all is vanity
The devil has become the highest bidder on a soul that
was sold for cheap
We, the people, operate through small limited views
when there is always a bigger picture present
What is your price?
In some way, shape, or form...
we all pay a price
What is your price for love?
...to be accepted?
...for companionship?
You could be desperately pursuing the enemy
to eat, sleep, commune with, hang out with...
many have and will continue to overlook the fact that
Jesus is the "purchaser" of the soul
We were bought with a price that is above and goes far
beyond a dollar amount
The ransom required bloodshed
therefore, our lives don't really belong to us
we are only leasing them
You don't even own the breath that you breathe
or the heart that you can feel beating in your chest
Repentance is needed to be reconciled
unto ELOHIYM, our Father
The Internal Revenue Service has nothing on Him
He is coming to collect that which we owe

Cornelius P. Thomas Jr.

Are you selling yourself for true purpose or vanity?
I have chosen to surrender and "sell out" to YAH'S way
Mock me if you will
I know a wise investment when I see it
I am wealthy towards AHBA
Prosperous in the earth and I have treasures
in heaven
Angels on call
dispatched as I use my secret weapon
coupled with praise and confessions
Worship is essential
we cannot welcome the Most High on our terms
He doesn't dwell in unclean temples
In some way, shape, or form…
we all pay a price
What is yours?

HIDDEN

The Kingdom of YAH is spoken in a mystery
hidden from the natural comprehension of the mind
Every day, the battle is between dumbing down to
worldly systems or embracing Kingdom principles
Hidden wisdom has been ordained for those chosen
before the worlds were framed
The deep and intricate things of ELOHIYM
are revealed unto us by His Spirit

Prophetic utterances are documented
hidden although made simple and plain
One's natural eyes and ears can deceive them
end up running this race called *life* in vain
Jesus has defeated all sin and death
call it debt cancellation
He died to become our emancipation
death could not defeat the transformation

ELOHIYM'S children are hidden
from the comprehension levels of the world
Elected, selected, ordained, and trained
right before their very eyes
Still, they fail to comprehend
the truth is hidden
The Word was made flesh
The ancient powers that be hijacked the historical
context, white washed the entire story
in order to establish dominance

Cornelius P. Thomas Jr.

However, this Living Word was never bound
by the crafty counsel of men
The heavens and the earth were framed
by that same Word
Yet, He was overlooked, despised, rejected
…and ultimately crucified
Lynched on the behalf of carrying out a
divine assignment
One must lose their life for the sake of sacrifice
in order to follow Him
We await the coming Kingdom
looked upon as foolish

A bad apple can spoil the bunch
this means some fruit is forbidden
Many will embrace their "common sense"
while the Holy Spirit who knows all remains hidden
Robbed out of the true value of life
clinging to emotions and intellect
When a divine nature is embraced and a divine order is
established in one's life, faith, Holy Spirit, emotions,
and intellect can all work together

However, the true message of the gospel and salvation
remains hidden from blinded eyes
Words of power and authority are ridiculed
all because "they say" it's the "white man's religion"

THE INTENT TO EDIFY

Wise men lay up knowledge
but the mouth of the foolish is near destruction
Although it sounds foolish to my flesh,
I find glory in my infirmities
YAH'S strength is made perfect in my weakness
I have grown to respect tribulation
Pressure, suffering, persecution, and abandonment
will cause you to grow
There is a lesson to be learned in all things
The present sufferings have an expiration date
what is today must come to pass
I had to get delivered from man's opinion
Chasing destiny…
longing to please the Father
We all have imperfections
Is this a valid excuse not to strive for perfection?
Every day that I awake, I realize that YAHUAH
has graced me with another day to draw closer unto Him
The Holy Spirit is not to be grieved or quenched
YAHUSHA is the way, the truth, and the life
By Him, all things exist and are made possible
circumstances are temporary
The devil's threat has been demolished
by revelation knowledge
Nothing can remove the Elect out of YAH'S hand
…except for the blatant rebellion of the Elect
We can willingly jump out of His hand
no man can boast in the election

Cornelius P. Thomas Jr.

It is a mandate from the heavens that doesn't require
permission from mankind
Satan can transform into an angel of light
we must seek a discernment of spirits
to identify his informants
They will always attempt to pervert
what YAH has ordained as sacred
The war from the beginning has always been about
knowledge and illumination
From the days of the fallen angels teaching men…
until the wickedness of this present day…
It's all about information
supposedly secret
If you possess a spiritual eye to peep it
you'll notice the battles are strategic
My intent to edify
allows the pen to testify
My mission is to provoke thought
you do the research to find the lies

THE INK BLEEDS

Life comes with different levels
tests and lessons
Life cannot be defined or summed up
by one's opinion
It is amazing how so many people tend to get stuck in a
certain area, level, or period of their lives
Traumatic experiences, prior tragedies
…past or present pain
The future can become stained
by heartaches, broken vows, or strongholds
Satan enters through open doors of vulnerability
The devil desires to limit your future
won't allow you to forget your past
The clock never stops ticking
How can we race against time?
I abide under the shadow of EL SHADDAI
The Creator of Time
So since "time" is on my side,
I choose to use it wisely
YAH can see through the eyes of eternity
I can remember the dark days
mentally dwelling in a cave
Sin and circumstance's slave
couldn't seem to shake the wicked ways
Heavily sedated in a daze
countless years of feeling hopeless
I answered the call and surrendered my all
when YAH apprehended my focus
Deep emotional ties to the struggle

Cornelius P. Thomas Jr.

a lion in the jungle
Attacks are launched from every angle
free spirits remain humble
…and what of life?
Life cannot be defined or summed up
by one's opinion
Different paths are traveled which will ultimately
lead to one of two destinations
There are decisions to be made
fiery trials and tribulations
I am ignited to overcome ignorance
and curse oppression at the root
Life comes with different levels
tests and lessons
Who can silence the desire for change?
Procrastination and isolation
can cause the truth to look strange
Who really wants to hear the truth?
Souls are misguided
eyes are blinded
Wisdom is provided
yet, many cannot find it
The expressions from my heart
laced with an undeniable passion
Is sure to reach the heart
in an unreliable fashion…
is how mankind continues to operate
YAH'S mercy is extended
today there's a chance to rebuild
The great awakening is for a remnant
He will hear the cries of those oppressed

Product of America

I am connected through the Spirit of Truth
My pen had an adverse reaction
forced to strategize and execute
We believe to receive
we conceive to achieve
Until I reach my place of rest
the ink will continue to bleed

Cornelius P. Thomas Jr.

EPIDEMIC IN THE WILDERNESS
Jeremiah 17:4

The media will never portray our true culture
in a positive light
That doesn't fit in with the crafty counsel,
the agenda, the narrative
A wealth of wisdom and knowledge is laid up
in the revelation of Jesus Christ
Greatness can come from the people and places
that you least expect
Talents are not the issue
the people are destroyed for a lack of knowledge
…failing to recognize the assignment on earth
The identity crisis versus God given gifts
and talents
Wickedness and righteousness are two opposite paths
or lifestyles that will never attract
Hidden potential is constantly overlooked
in an aimless manner
Exposed weaknesses strip the human's control
therefore, many will fail to cry out for help
Not willing to take a loss today
in exchange for gain tomorrow
He that is slothful in his work is a brother to him
that is great waster
The lost generation
embraces a microwave process
Most of us want results fast
and we want them now
Therefore, the masses have turned to destruction

Product of America

possessing itching ears that are dull of hearing when it
comes to the truth
In the wilderness trying to find our way
can't see the eagles for vultures
perverting and redefining culture
The question is, *"Whose definition of culture?"*
The truth or what we were made to believe
*Who will embrace originality that will complement their
individuality?*
Some of us are foreign to hard work
not willing to roll up our sleeves
The men can't walk in true purpose
too busy trying to be G's
Our perception, the devil deceives
through radio and TV
This encourages us to settle for less
instead of doing our best
We become occupied with making excuses
foreigners to true success
Everyone dresses the same!
All of the slang is the same!
Instead of calling on our Savior's name
many will stay blind in search of fame
Nevertheless, greatness can come from people
and places that you least expect
I see plenty of talents without vision
bound by the devil's threat
Gifts that will be wasted due to no
knowledge of purpose
They say the good die young
the kids are angry and plagued by curses

Cornelius P. Thomas Jr.

Dying too fast
with no respect for the dash
Illiterate managers of finances
exploited slaves for cash
Gun shots rang out in the dark corners
of the wilderness
Darkness and ignorance tends to complement
one another
YAHUAH, Creator of all, can heal us
from this epidemic
Knowledge is only powerful once it has been applied
I know two epidemic twins named
"Laziness" and "Waste"
YAH provided the antidote
two twins named "Mercy" and "Grace"
*Who is willing to get focused in order to overcome
the rat race?*
The modern day Promised Land is waiting
but, you must have an acquired taste

AT A STANDSTILL

Weary years
silent tears
Lord, you hear our inner cries
adversities define true soldiers
Therefore, I lift YAH'S name on high
The struggle will continue
the movement will remain alive

These are ballads of a foreign soldier
Will we ever overcome mediocrity?
Spiritual and racist oppression
foreknown and predestined to walk
in the paths of the upright
One day we'll rest from our labor
but, this day we must fight

The strength of the oppressed
quiet prayers of the down trodden
Fear is overcome by faith and courage
faith pleases the Almighty
Determination will overcome laziness
light always overthrows the darkness
Opposition comes to overtake
naysayers will continue to underrate

If YAH be for us
He is more than the world against us
The powers of darkness cannot decide our fate
weary years, silent tears

Cornelius P. Thomas Jr.

Lord, you hear our inner cries
ballads of a foreign soldier
Singing praises unto YAH until the demise

There is hope for a better day
love can smother the unquenchable flames of hatred
Toxic words pierce through the heart of a dreamer
words can become murder weapons
I carry the memories of many influential forefathers
in my heart
Faith emerges
within the silent chambers of isolation
The blood of all of the warriors from the struggle
has been injected into my veins
Overshadowed by the blood of Jesus Christ
the chief cornerstone
I am more than a conqueror

I visualize former slaves singing and working
in the fields
Crying out to their Father in heaven
to avenge them of their enemies

Today, there's still so much hatred, rebellion,
and shattered dreams among the ghetto youths
How can we not embrace the truth?
Discrimination is now more subtle and strategic
I view the complicated picture of equality
The scales are still not balanced
Yet, many will view scripture from the oppressor's
vantage point and never discover how this all came to be

Product of America

Repentance is needed
submission to the Holy Spirit
Instead of feeding the thief
we need to seek the Prince of Peace
Will we ever overcome mediocrity?
Stuck at a standstill and most of the wounds
are self-inflicted

Cornelius P. Thomas Jr.

A CONSTANT STRUGGLE

Boys become men
based on the things that we go through
The decisions that are made
life will constantly show you
uncertainty
We have to take responsibility
and continuously forsake
unproductive activities

Life itself is a mystery
one big poem
Constantly in need of direction
I ask YAH to establish my goings
The struggle never stops
at times, it really hurts to see
Tribulations show up
but we need adversity
Part of the freedom process
a continual process
Some are foreigners to overall progress
constantly chasing a profit

Tribulation brings me to the realization
that time waits for no man
We must discern times and seasons
and for the Kingdom, take a stand
Wisdom on handling situations
are provided by God's design
Through the transformation process

Product of America

one's beauty is defined
Although, the phases are dreaded
trying times ignite this freedom writer
Like wine that gets better with time
trials can produce a seasoned fighter
My weapons are no longer carnal
fleeing from the normal picture
Hoping for what I see not
standing on the Holy Scriptures

I was in a rush to become a grown man
the growth was based on the physical
The real war is spiritual
so the Holy Spirit had to improve my visual
In order to become lyrical
the struggle continues
This is only the beginning
payback for all of the hell that I've been through
My friends are few
I choose to take destiny by the hand
When everyone else walks away
a real man will still stand

When boys become men
they will shed the excess weight
I used to blame others for my mistakes
Now, I utilize the 24 hours of the day
No time to hang with the fellas
if they're not focused on advancing
Embracing leadership skills to maneuver
through the circumstances

Cornelius P. Thomas Jr.

A real man believes in his Creator
He will disregard outside opinions
It is a constant struggle
journeying through different dimensions
The struggle doesn't define me
the struggle refines me
Carrying my cross to follow the *"Boss"*
forgetting all that's behind me

INTRICATE PLOTS

YAH wouldn't have led me to the pond
if there were no fish in it
Inside of the last hours
have to make the most of every minute
The Day of Judgment is at hand
it is approaching, getting closer
Holding my stance as a soldier
before the day is over
As the sun is going down
we find the strength to carry on
All of the "so called" friends are gone
left me with my heart torn

By the Holy Spirit I'm drawn
to that secret place of intimacy
Demonic spirits try to diminish me
but the heart of a warrior beats intricately
The most fragile, yet strongest part of me
is my determination
Holy Spirit is my *Ambassador*
in Him I find strength

*How can scattered pieces of a puzzle come together to
frame a perfect picture?*
Longing for deep riches that are hidden
within Godly wisdom
My thoughts tend to weep
but dreams to make an impact flow freely

Cornelius P. Thomas Jr.

Ballads of a foreign soldier
chosen to be a joint-heir with Christ
Held captive by a burning passion to know my
Heavenly Father on the next level
His grace that is upon me
continues to silence the critics
His uncommon favor continues to pierce through
the soul of he who doubts
There is no confidence within my flesh
so I'm left standing without
a physical support system

Yet, I embrace the love that I feel from the few
the love that the Father has for me is unfailing
It will stand the test of time because
He is the Creator of it
I embrace this love affair in private
and stand bold as a lion in public
Separated from the common and familiar
…and all that I thought I knew
Then I was executed
introduced to the newness of life

Now, they with whom I used to play
learned to scheme with…
Built a team with…
dared to dream with
They search for me among the old
not knowing that I died and started the journey of
transformation, had to ditch the grave clothes
YAH wouldn't have led me to the pond

Product of America

if there were no fish in it
He wouldn't have allowed me to start the journey
if I wasn't able to finish
…and so I strike relentless
While exposing the truest part of me
intricate plots unfold
Prophetic words of artistry
still, we must go deeper

Cornelius P. Thomas Jr.

THE STORY TELLER

Come and pick the mind of a story teller
look into the eyes of the resilient
A Kingdom builder mistaken for a rebel
tired of mediocre levels
Where do we go from here?
Shed so many ghetto tears
many of us haven't even begun to live
The pain that I feel
is because the struggle is too real
Training grounds become breeding grounds
I cannot afford to chill

Some may get it twisted
yeah, I'm seated in heavenly places with Christ
Have to get off of high horses to get in the trenches
to possibly save someone else's life

So many have lost their lives
so many have missed the signs
Let's examine strategic operations
the system's design
They constantly pimp the poor
and urge the rich to get richer
Even many modern day churches are perverted
What is wrong with this picture?
Effective lyrics of poetry is what I deliver
with hopes to deliver
Called to provoke thought which leads to freedom
in this action packed thriller

Product of America

Sitting on the shore of the river
posted up under a tree
Had to sprint to a quiet spot to worship YAH
the natural realm is filled with captivity

The story teller…
suffers long to provide the script
Who is present to listen in and soak up
this free gift?
Freely given to those who receive it
however, I sacrifice to write
An empathic verbal assassin
I can feel the people's pain and the wicked device

Would love to provide poetry filled
with birds, bees, and trees
But, there's a burden to document this Word
the Savior can set people free
I represent a *Miracle Worker*
had to come to the realization
That many people don't possess faith
to effectively stand in tribulation
I sip from the well of Living Waters
staying in my lane as an instrument of change
Come and pick the mind of a story teller
sure to represent as it was ordained

Cornelius P. Thomas Jr.

THINK OUTSIDE OF THE BOX

Passion is likened to intense emotional drive
that is in need of balance
Meaning its effects can stem from good or evil
structure is needed to cultivate gifts and talents
Faith can see the invisible
and accomplish the impossible
Fear has crippled countless individuals
it can blind your optical and magnify obstacles
Do you possess fear or faith?
Why settle for less and play it safe?
Why do people allow life's issues to push them into a
place of submission?
Yet, many of us continue to fight a fight
that we cannot win
Who can contend with Almighty God?
Who can overthrow what has already been written in the
sacred Scriptures?
Many will forsake heaven's call in an attempt
to take ownership of their lives
With God lies the knowledge of witty inventions
…the hidden secrets of true purpose
Faith is simply choosing to believe Him
despite the temporary odds and circumstances
We must flee from the islands of what we deem
as safe in our limited minds
Fear is in the unknown
but every living being will reap a harvest
from the seeds that are sown
Instead of heeding the call to be radical

some will settle, complain, and live life unfulfilled
We all have an appointment with death
Why not take productive risks on the battlefield?
That risk may be the key to unlock your destiny
on this journey
Life is for living
there is no way we can rehearse it
There is a purpose perfect for you
although no human being is perfect
There is such a thing as a perfect fit
…like a tailor-made suit
Many view the Holy Spirit as some creepy trance
that the church mothers go into to shout and dance
That is a misrepresentation…
He is the Inventor of Creativity
He provides wise counsel
that is normally found outside of the box
of human intellect
We could never out-think this Sovereign Spirit
life is uncertain but you may want to consider allowing
Him to reconstruct your thought pattern
and deliver you from the box of normalcy
Purpose, passion, and destiny are waiting
choose wisely

Cornelius P. Thomas Jr.

OVERTHROW LIMITATIONS

Self-doubt is a disease that can keep
generations bound by limitations
However, there are no boundaries that cannot be crossed
as we follow the leadership of the Holy Spirit
I have chosen to adhere to ELOHIYM'S plan
for my life
Poetry in motion
exposes hope for the hopeless
Words Spirit and life
that can cause one to redirect or regain focus

YAH will maintain
that which He has ordained
If I can touch a wounded soul
I'll forever go against the grain
Every day, I expect the *Miracle Worker* to work
on the behalf of His children
Those laced with the grace of resilience can stand amidst
persecution, ridicule, trouble and opinions
Any and everything contrary to the faith-walk

The devil tries to oppress YAH'S people
because he fears the faith connection
His power is stripped once we truly tap into the power of
Christ, which was freely given unto us
There is nothing impossible
to he or she who believes
My job is to ignite mountain movers
the gifted and talented individuals who cannot be

Product of America

contained by the box of the system
Although, sometimes we feel like victims
we can shout the victory
Halleluyah and all praises to The Most High
the price was paid for us to walk in victory
Mentally climbing the highest mountains
hurdling over obstacles
By faith, we can speak to the mountains
and prepare to witness the impossible
The enemy cannot silence the voice
of the pure Spirit
Purpose will not be contaminated
by these sideline critics

The people who surround you
will influence what you can accomplish
False friends and dead weight
can keep the mind's state at a limit
Faith is acting on what one believes
to be true
Many creative minds have become sedated due to
paralysis by analysis
...not following their "first mind" or that
"gut feeling"
Obsessive thinking can lead to self-doubt
true identities can only be found
in the *Creator of all living*

Demonic spirits capitalize
off of the identity crisis of men
Darkness and ignorance tend to complement

one another
However, a renewed mind is unstoppable
the true Light will continue to shine
Any and everything that resembles limitations
shouldn't possess your attention or time
I AM a magnet to good success
I curse the bondage of restrictions and limitations
in every area of our lives in the name of
Jesus

Behind Enemy Lines

Cornelius P. Thomas Jr.

CHOOSING TO BE MORE

Inadequacy is in the back of me
made a decision to elevate
Mind, body, and spirit
the devil always comes to separate
YAHUAH whispers in my ear
the authority from heaven I delegate
Prejudice and limitations are in the hearts of men
we mentally segregate
Instead of choosing to eliminate
a limited or negative mental state
And not follow trends but innovate
we allow Satan to infiltrate
Because, we don't display Godly faith
I'm flipping the script today
I have to live with the consequences of my decisions
therefore, I trust in YAH'S way

We're not foreign to tribulation
well acquainted with imitations
Men barely want the heat of leadership
but will criticize and judge a leader's frustrations
Promise breaking…
a common falsehood among brothers
If YAH blesses me with wisdom
my job is to spread knowledge to others
The real truth is hated
because spiritual liberty is celebrated
By mankind, I'm underrated
but determination, they can't break it

Product of America

Mankind is controlled by the spirit world
some embrace fiction and deny the facts
even when I stumble in foreign territory
YAH'S mercy keeps me bouncing back
Call it the grace of God
therefore, I seek the face of God
Idolatry is great in this wicked land
I bet they can't replace my God

Procreation, mind elevation
and transformations are mine
They will witness the supernatural revelation
from the manifestation of countless rhymes

Cornelius P. Thomas Jr.

A WEALTH OF KNOWLEDGE

Opportunities to flourish are in operation
building a legacy for the coming generations
Self discovery and self mastery is continual education
the real starting point to victory is salvation
Too much deceptive information
the powers that be mock at the people's ignorance
Many times, we labor for the wrong things
pursue vain paths with diligence
They say violence isn't justified
however, I murder the lack of effort
Everyone won't receive the freedom of the truth
we can want it for them, but they have to want better

The warfare is psychological,
chemical, and biological
Branches connected to a spiritual root
the entire tree is diabolical
Allow your minds to travel with me
as I provoke thought within the lyrics
Critics come a dime a dozen
try the spirits by the Spirit
To see if I was sent from the Higher Power
all praises to EL ELYON
Better to please God than man
man will switch quicker than a playlist full of songs

Forefathers pushed for integration
just like ancient Israel asked the Prophet for a king
When they were already in the best position

Product of America

our decisions cause us to suffer from plots and schemes
Just like an abusive marriage
the wife wants to be treated just and fairly
Her husband is a narcissist who promises to
do better but, his words will rarely…
Match his actions
he offers perks that make it hard for her to leave
The abuse continues and become normal
this has been our reality for centuries, still no ease

Then, once the scales begin to fall from your eyes
you come to find the relationship is adulterous
You broke covenant with your Heavenly Father
His Christ is the true husbandman, they're insulting us
Our appetites became gluttonous
filled with idolatry and whoredom
So we are treated as such, we honor material possessions,
prestige and super stardom
This American dream became a nightmare
because it never included us
If they were serious about change
they would revisit the Constitution, which excluded us
Instead they gave us pagan worship intertwined
throughout these religions
Their education, their double standards
the illusion of inclusion and division
I provide a wealth of knowledge that
supersedes any dollar amount
Hope we can get free from this mental matrix
wisdom is greater than a dollar amount
Wake up!

Cornelius P. Thomas Jr.

AWAKE THE SLEEPING GIANT
Ezekiel 37

I have Biblical rights
the Kingdom is revealed as I write
Melanin flows throughout this shell
a spirit being whose vessel will ignite
To awake the sleeping giant
that the giants of oppression may fall
The people are handicapped by limitations
sick of having to crawl
If one of us can chase a thousand
two of us can chase ten
Unified by the bond of peace
a divine release is within

Faith can move mountains
we've suffered hardships and still counting
The devil divides to conquer
in flood waters, many are drowning
We must put the demons to flight
situations ignite the revolution
Submit and allow the Ruach to lead us
YAHUSHA is the best solution
He's demanding restitution
spiritual reparations for the down trodden
In the secret place of preparation
guaranteed to rise from the bottom

So much has happened
there's still more to come

Product of America

Faith requires action
let YAH'S will be done
He's hope for the hopeless in this
beginning of sorrows
Degraded outlooks, broken spirits
in a worser state tomorrow
So many have passed away
I've lost count on naming them
So many problems throughout my life
I got fed up with claiming them

We must confess what the Word says
I expect miracles, signs, and wonders
I speak life in death's valley
and hold my stance as an overcomer
The power of the Spirit is within me
have to call it out of my belly
The Word stepped out on nothing and created something
How can they tell me?
That the unseen realm isn't real
victory is on the battlefield
We have to march into the enemy's camp
and overcome he who steals

Awake the sleeping giant
that the giants of oppression may fall
Time to seek new revelation
stick to following heaven's call
EL wants to use us as instruments
life is no coincidence
It all happens by design

Cornelius P. Thomas Jr.

the Light shines by intelligence
So much confusion in this world
word curses and negative chitter chatter
Some are screaming *Black Lives Matter*
some are screaming *Blue Lives Matter*
We're desensitized to true love
hatred will cause one to live barbaric and hard
Some are more worried about going viral
phones are always handy to record…
Their neighbors in distress
altercations and mess
Pandemics causing the masses to walk in fear
YAH has the final say and He's not done yet

Love is the foundation for effective
righteous living
An awakening and healing is needed
deliverance from these mental prisons
A spiritual cleansing is at hand
consecration and sanctification
ELOHIYM is still holy
and He's calling for His Holy nation
To wake up, rise up
hold your stance in these evil days
Our *Redemption* is drawing near
fear can't stand in the eyes of faith
There's an army rising up
no longer will they be able to divide us
Intercession is our greatest weapon
the enemy knows that his time is up

IT TAKES FAITH

Jealousy is in the land
extending a helping hand to sisters and brothers
As a whole, we're on the list of extinction
somehow we must recover
Mediocre drama smothers…
visualizing past peers in a coffin
Diluted mental states
the hate shows up often

In a desert place, the valley
the devil desires to have me
In a dungeon, the wilderness
my flesh, YAH is killing it
The pressure is building up
having thoughts of giving up
On this paper, I'm found spilling guts
in the natural, it can get really rough

The power is within my gut
sometimes a struggle to stand
In the midst of uncertain seasons
trusting God in a dry land
I can see the promise from afar
on foreign soil, seeing cop cars
Having sacred visions of the *Promised Land*
this genocide is a constant war
Filled with demonic suggestion
feel more like an enemy than a citizen
Binding and rebuking depression

Cornelius P. Thomas Jr.

loosing peace, prosperity, and discipline
Heartache is seen on the faces
I've witnessed eyes that lost the twinkle
Until the eye is full of light and single
it's not really safe to mingle
One moment, we're up
the next second, we're down
An emotional rollercoaster
trying to get to the top of the mound

The secret is to disregard the things that are temporal
seen with the natural eye
Racing towards a spiritual pinnacle
…to a land that is plentiful
The *Word of YAH* is commendable
blessings can be obtained in the here and now
He will make a way somehow

It takes faith to win the race
unbelief disqualifies
Without faith, it's impossible to please YAH
actions are required after the tears we cry
Feeding on the living scripture
anything else please reconsider
Time is perfectly orchestrated
the Spirit is speaking as I gaze at the river
It takes faith to win the race
don't allow your hope to become misplaced
Blessings can be obtained today
we must be led the right way

WISDOM IS

Wisdom is not found
within the clothes that I wear
Just like a woman's beauty is not
determined by her hair
The recital is tribal
a representation of the Savior
Survival is vital
the blueprint is welcomed by the paper
My culture is lost and holds no significance
this is what they suggest
Originality is not the mentality
so most will continue to fail the test

Every protest has a cause
comprehension levels are filled with flaws
Success shouldn't be determined by the limelight
human notoriety and applause
My eyes are consumed with grief
seems like the storms of life are trying to take us out
YAH'S compassion is higher than human intellect
delivered me from the lion's mouth
Metaphorically
destruction is waiting for those who forsake their help
The Savior can be touched by our infirmities
He knows the pain that is felt

The strategies, the agony, the last to breathe
the man in me
Solitary insanity

Cornelius P. Thomas Jr.

chaos dwells among humanity
YAH gave us the gift of life
we all slip in this life
Wisdom allows one to get a grip
and distinguish between wrong and right
I own the right…
to forsake all and follow Christ
With no confidence in man
his heart can grow as cold as ice
My well-being is in the hands of another
depending on the Almighty
I possess faith and a dream
also weaknesses and temptations to entice me

Probably a million others like me
some are scared to admit the struggle
To hell with trying to uphold a false image
my eyes have witnessed so much trouble
the definition of life
…or deposition to life
Comes with a schedule precise
embrace the recognition of life
Wisdom is not found
within the clothes that I wear
Represent by example
ELOHIYM is there amidst the warfare

POWERFUL PEN

This powerful pen
comes after sorrowful men
Seek God's plan today and tomorrow
we'll win
Helping hands understand
that we had to borrow from friends
I have wisdom to lend
I first had to follow the trends

The wise man has played the fool
despised and ridiculed
Decided to dream big and speak
to the mountains for them to move
There's no way that we can lose
if we choose to interact with the Creator
Powerful pens and the *Creative Breath*
intricate thoughts for an innovator
It is written…
that the Lamb of YAH was smitten
Rejected of men
betrayed and snake bitten

Too many hate missions
the venom of false friends
The choices that are made today
will eventually cost in the end
Expectations are lost in the wind
hope is within the clock's ticking
Salvation, healing, and deliverance

Cornelius P. Thomas Jr.

is within the Savior that has risen
We have to let the haters hate
just decide not to listen
Direction is better than speed
if YAH is in the lead position
To hell with the opposition
that is his final destination
So he sedates the minds of mankind
to join his eternal vacation

Too much procrastination
and separation is in this land
If we don't put the issues aside
How can unity stand and make demands?
The power from heaven is held up
we often buy what the evil spirits sell us
Their chief is the author of confusion
the *Prince of Peace* will never fail us
The days are filled with evil
tribulations will expose the soul
Sorrow has taken over regions
but the pen refuses to fold

Controlled by the Holy Ghost
separated for the song in my notes
I believe that there is freedom in these letters
revelation's overflow
This powerful pen
comes after sorrowful men
Seek God's plan today and tomorrow
we'll win

Product of America

FOLLOW THE LEADER

"Holy Spirit, I need You
to rule, reign, and abide
Where I will cease to be
within Your power I can hide
In the secret place, I'll reside
rely on You to lead and guide
Me on this righteous path and enhance
my poetic vibe."

A wicked and adulterous generation
the vultures are penetrating
Instigating, imitating
the positive images are fading…
Away
the night turns back into day
In lamentation, flesh amputation
faults confessed as I pray
Outside, I can hear the sirens screaming
every corner there's a different demon
The closest of friends have separated
the author of confusion came between us
Said some things we didn't mean but…
YAHUSHA has redeemed us
From the curse in the earth
His blood was shed to clean us

The wounds of a friend are faithful
covetous intentions are hateful
How can you distinguish between the two?

Cornelius P. Thomas Jr.

The conclusion could end up fatal
I'll use my faith to
praise my way to my breakthrough
I long for more of the Living EL
some are satisfied and make due
In tune with YAHUAH-ELOHIYM
I could never let go of dreams
Urged to let go of things
everything that doesn't profit me

The joy floods my soul
every thug that I know...
Have a hard time understanding
I remain separated for the canvas
The parchments of paper
to document life's events deemed as major
They flee from the truth
only Jesus can save you
This is why I seek that hiding place
He is constantly providing space
These wicked times are getting harder to take
the judgment for this world is great

On these scripts I meditate
by faith, I'm urged to testify
Who can enter into judgment with God?
No flesh can be justified
As I continue to go deeper
the days become sweeter
Planted by the rivers of water as I
follow the Leader

PRISONER OF UNSPOKEN WORDS

Day in and day out
praying for the light of Christ to shine
Through me, sometimes limited
held captive by my mind
As I study the hypocrisy
of the system's design
They hate me without a cause
truly the sign of the times
Hated for trusting YAH
labeled by the color of my skin
My household family is depending on me
so many trials and predicaments

The Lamb's blood is innocent
He gave His life for humanity
Feels like I'm one step away
from my breakthrough or insanity
These spirits attack randomly
forced to grow through the trouble
Visualizing a perfect picture
many pieces are in this complicated puzzle
Life is one big pattern
an uncertain journey
I constantly have to sift through empty words
fleeing from issues that doesn't concern me
A prisoner of unspoken words
a broken heart and personal thoughts
I have faith and a dream
also weaknesses and faults

Cornelius P. Thomas Jr.

Imprisoned by gravity
limited motions and movements
Relocated to maximum security
tested and proven
Protected by mighty angels
handcuffed by this Holy Spirit
Turbulence is in the air
trouble expressed in the lyrics
In search of my piece of the pie
as this earth yields her increase
A piece of mind, a piece of the Rock
and comfort from the Prince of Peace

Can't trust no one or nothing
without consent from the Almighty
YAH has placed boundaries that man can't cross
so I hold on to the promises tightly
Countless tears have been shed
dead weight has been shed
The seasons of testing we dread
premature actions we regret

I await the manifestation from the prophetic realm
as the predator hunts his prey
Every messenger has their day
I'm a passenger, YAH leads the way
The Light shines in the darkness
trouble ignited creativity within the artist
I will stand regardless
and hold my post like a war vet

PROPHETIC SIGNS

Eradication
of the countless years of aggravation
The wickedness of man
is to my soul, an agitation
Without the acceptance of Jesus
there's no way that we can possibly make it
The Lord observes wicked imaginations
before Him we stand naked
A refugee in a foreign land
a stranger due to YAH'S election
Repenting for the time that was wasted
today I seek correction

A prisoner of the earth
until my King calls me home
Cannot overstep the boundaries of His command
in the trenches is where I roam
Crying out for sanctification
in need of consecration
Seeking to get the most out of this journey
plagued by spiritual and mental segregation

I possess the power of the Sovereign YAH
determination makes me strong
Contemporary society could care less
stereotyped by the color of my skin tone
I must keep keeping on
my closest friends don't even know me
There's a constant death for me

Cornelius P. Thomas Jr.

lured to dwell in the Holy of Holies
The blood of the Lamb covers me
we don't have a clue about His power
I AM at my best
a success even in this same hour
Sweet dreams can turn sour
if I wait on my neighbors to cosign
They can't see the vision like I see
forced to pay the critics no mind

They can't comprehend the warning signs
taking place at the rising of the sun
Naysayers speak against the peculiar people
overtaken by the viper's tongue
I seek to perfect it
an abundant life found in the message
Hoping for what I see not
no boundaries are in the secret place where I'm headed

Praying that I may decrease
and keep the devil under my feet
Embracing discernment in the fiery furnace
until I get free
Learning to welcome the trials
rather than run from them and live in denial
YAH wrote the script that is unfolding
so I can rest and make time for the worthwhile
The poetic style is versatile
as long as my soul is the opposite of empty
Stories are exposed and easily told
because the Holy Spirit lives within me

Product of America

Eradication
of the countless years of aggravation
Overwhelmed by YAH'S visitation
can't utter some of the sacred revelations
Love has waxed cold and the times
are far from kind
Behold the poetry lines
will reveal the prophetic signs

Cornelius P. Thomas Jr.

BEHIND ENEMY LINES

Rejoice oh ye Heavens
because ELOHIYM reigns
He unfolds the plans of life
victory is in His Son's name
Spiritual mysteries are revealed
prophecies will be fulfilled
On this foreign battlefield
tribulations birth a worship that is real
Immoral blood spills
the Holy Prophets are killed
The past is based upon prior tragedies
today has a chance to rebuild

War tactics documented
in a raw form of the poetic
Uttering parables prophetic
praying that lost souls will grasp and get it
YAH-ELOHIYM is all powerful
He releases the anointing to flow through His messengers
Sanitize your inner circle
and flee from unfruitful passengers
Soldiers must follow commandments and guidelines
because this world has no rules
This is why demons are running rampant
people are misused and abused

The spirit world is very active
when the RUACH is present
we can't be passive

Product of America

Souls are on the line
time is our greatest asset
In this act of war
men turn to sin and switch sides
Betrayal is in operation behind the scenes
seducing spirits lie
A fight for territory
every day is a constant battle
My weapons are not carnal
the inner man and mental capacity is what I rattle

Demonic spirits travel
laboring, competing with angels
The Holy Spirit has the dominion to execute
the power to transform or change us
The Lamb of YAH was slain
Jesus is His name
Our Father is a Consuming Fire
baptized in eternal flames…
are the wicked, the explicit
and those foreign to the truth
Hell fire is a continual torment
however, there are many confused views

This is a spiritual warfare
between truth seekers and thieves
Nevertheless, the *Elect of YAH* were ordained
for times such as these
A lost generation
burned out from dehydration
Continuous decision making

Cornelius P. Thomas Jr.

reservations for an eternal vacation
In a race against time
they don't observe prophetic signs
Memories of a foreign war
the chosen are fighting behind enemy lines

We shall overcome by the blood of the Lamb
and the words of our testimony
We trust in the *Lion of the tribe of Judah*
we love not our lives unto the death
YAHUAH has ordered our steps
by His grace we are kept

THE REMNANT

We've been nominated
to possess the land and dominate it
Abraham is the founder of the promise
the blood of the living Christ exonerated
Validated mankind
only if man accepts Him
Started with the lost sheep of Israel
we must honor and respect Him
The Sovereign YAH
Creator of all that is living
Father of the elect
thankful for the grace that has been given

He has established the Body for Kingdom business
we must be cleansed, purification
The devil has power to bless with the hopes to
blind to lure us from the destination
Sanctification…
comes through the daily process structure
The closer we draw to the Most High
satanic attacks will get tougher

As we go through the proper channels
and climb to different faith levels
Principalities, assigned demons
then we come face to face with the devil
The anointing of the Ruach is upon us
that we may carry out YAH'S purpose
Christ disarmed the power of the enemy

Cornelius P. Thomas Jr.

He redeemed us from the curses
Everyone wants to go to heaven
but don't want to take the chance
We have power to bring Heaven to earth
and speak the Word over the circumstance
There are a few that are willing to go against the grain
determined to go all the way
Drawing strength as we pray
from the commandments we will not sway

Looking towards that greater day
when this corruptible body is changed
Our identities are enhanced by the blood
our focus has been rearranged
Disciplined with radical behavior
true purpose mixed with passion
Faith is more than just belief
but using belief to take action

I'm thankful for emotional stability
as well as spiritual growth
Ordinary people with limitations will not
experience the places that we will go
Willing to die for this cause
Christ has called us as His wife
There's no greater love than this
the man laid down His life
It takes a sacrifice
Who is willing to pay the price?
I rejoice in YAH'S mercy and grace
…part of the remaining trace

IMPRISONED BY GRAVITY

So much murder in this land
it's hard for the mourner to withstand
Unexplained pain
heaviness in a man's life span
Prisoner of the ink's tears
unspoken words, limited by gravity
Tormented by mental images
searching for clarity drastically

The system encourages oppression
violence in the hearts of the needy
Emotional trauma for countless mamas
compassion is mocked in the hearts of the greedy
Graveyards are full of wealth
full of broken dreams, but never full
The upright in heart is misunderstood
trampled underfoot because ears are dull

Fear and unbelief causes the inhabitants
to become gullible
They don't believe in miracles
even though YAH is incredible
The times are terrible
every man is in search of his portion
Some people murder with words, weapons,
or feticide… call it abortion
Everybody has played the fool
the dreamers suffer ridicule
So much unbelief and grief

Cornelius P. Thomas Jr.

compromising spirits are in the streets
Purposes become disappointed
frustration and broken homes
Broken families
aggression in the broken songs
Don't think it strange
the situations we go through
The tribulations that we grow through
to find the Christ faithful and true

Success will always depend
on one's determination
Time is not earned
so many will choose to waste it
We must get back to the basics
Jesus rebuilds the temple
Wisdom is sought after
creativity built on fundamentals

The days are filled with gloom
instead of seeking, some just assume
Only to come to the realization
that they're destined for doom
My Redemption is coming soon
dwelling in the midst of the wild
The various fiery trials
provoke these "Dear Diary files"
Walking the green mile
carrying sin's contraband
Laboring to produce good fruit in a
dry and barren land

Product of America

Mental dilemmas
the process is slow and simmer
In this microwave generation
everyone has their own agenda

Cornelius P. Thomas Jr.

THY WILL BE DONE

Babylon beware
the Kingdom of YAH is in the hearts of men
I AM the *house of prayer*
Sin causes Him to depart from men
but I need this love affair
Testimonies and the art within
they say favor isn't fair
Heavy burdens I don't have to bear

Urged to line up with the Word
the Rock of all ages
Speaking idle words is just absurd
when He can free minds from the cages
My dwelling place, my hiding place
my resting place, my secret place
Daily I welcome His leadership
within this strategic race

Find me standing on the promise
the grace of YAH is timeless
No wisdom greater than kindness
time is for defining
Through the tough times the rough rhymes
will penetrate corrupt minds
To destroy the yokes of bondage
the RUACH ELOHIYM abducts mine
My focus when it looks hopeless
depending on the supernatural
Offering YAH some praise

Product of America

although these days, it's not fashionable
Thought patterns are so rational
time to stand up like true radicals
YAH let thy will be done
I'm tired of flesh parading in the natural

"Let thy will be done
as it is in heaven
You're great and mighty
so we bow before Your presence.
Can't see the bigger picture
when we're going through
Despite it all
YAH we will follow You."

Trouble shows up often
from the cradle to the coffin
This closer walk is costing
forced to walk it like I talk it
Stage play of life no acting
have to stick and move with caution
The Resurrection and the Life
can revive a soul bound by exhaustion
Spiritually and mentally
He delivered me from past misery
In a world so fast paced
the rat race filled with trickery

He's my stability
even if man decides to turn from me
He will perfect that which is concerning me

Cornelius P. Thomas Jr.

I will glory in my infirmities

The EL of all creation
ever-present in situations
The trials and tribulations
different phases and stages
His faithfulness transcends
through barriers and trends
How can I blend in when I was
predestined to win?
His love will never fail
His Word shall prevail
Forever settled in heaven
the reason I can declare that all is well
Associated with the greatest
I never would have made it
Tunnel vision is required to follow the Messiah
on a path that is sacred

EXILED

The falling star shoots across the sky
an angel carries out the order
Speak the Word and dispatch angels
from the throne of the Father
Divine revelations
separation from tradition
Carrying the cross is the denial of self
ELOHIYM is not a magician
that works some magic trick
Casting demonic influence back to the pits
of hell, breaking the spell
to come up out of the abyss

Are we really leaders of society?
...or are we strategically hidden?
Cold shoulders in a cold world
will leave a soldier frost bitten
Exiled from the natural flow of things
compensated for my hunger and thirst
Endurance wins the race
into flames emotions burst
Only our faith can please YAH
and provoke Him to act on our behalf
The Ruach leads us on a lonely road
called the straight and narrow path

The government oppresses the people daily
impure motives come from hidden sin
Rejoicing in the sacrifice of my Savior

Cornelius P. Thomas Jr.

one day it will all come to an end
I'm a recipient of an everlasting covenant
partaker of a great inheritance
As long as we continue in the faith
for the Kingdom of YAH we represent
With such a resilience
through the dark hours we persevere
Fall down and get up
can't give up, the end is near
Stripped of sin's contraband
walking the green mile
Serving a life sentence
a prisoner of YAH exiled

INSIDE

Inside I'm inspired
because a lot of men died
Not fulfilling their dreams
instead living in between…
Pay periods
man the struggle is so serious
Driven by my ambitions
with the faith that makes them curious

Spectators speak about
desiring to see me without
Falling and their hands are not extended
reaching out
Can't afford to fake like a pretender
deep down I know that I'm a lender
Many will talk a good game
emotions get mixed up like a blender

Backed into a corner
determined at the bottom
Can't accept defeat and go under
consistency will always shock them
Worry tries to overtake me
it's connected to doubt
and doubt is connected to fear
Where do we go from here?

The heart and mind has to be clear
in order to hear YAH speaking

Cornelius P. Thomas Jr.

Attacks come subtle and sneaky
I refuse to let this defeat me
There is no peace treaty
in the midst of the spiritual war
Only Yahshua can reach me
the clay stretches so far

Out of place, out of socket
out of space like a rocket
The steps of a good man are ordered
guaranteed to prosper and profit
I reject the deposit
of the poisonous venom
ELOHIYM knows me in private
He allows me to keep the momentum

Ordained to stand through all of the suffering
the hardships and verbal murdering
No matter how the devil tries to plot
he cannot deter the dreams

Inside I'm inspired
because a lot of men died
Determined to keep it moving
feel my pain as the pen cries

WHAT CAN I OFFER?

I refuse to be held back
by depression, poverty, or lack
ELOHIYM doesn't slack
therefore, I'll reverse the attack
With a counter attack
fighting fire with spiritual flames
Satan will not limit my future
and consume it with pain
Ordained to maintain
my family is depending on me
I'm leaning on Everlasting Arms
would rather die than live phony

Sometimes my mind wonders and I get weary
a soldier dehydrated
My emotions do not control me
faith and peace infiltrated
YAH is my *Provider*
Why should I live in doubt or confinement?
Refuse to quit on this journey,
tailor-made mission and assignment
With faith, YAH can't ignore me
it is the opposite of worry
Faith helps me to compose my story
I can't be stopped because YAH is for me

As the world grows colder
this soldier's heart becomes softer
Understanding that the path of destruction is real

Cornelius P. Thomas Jr.

What can I offer?
I can offer prayer and support
Kingdom laced words of inspiration
Motivation to go places
and overthrow limitations
Just when they thought it was safe to say I quit
think again
The Holy Spirit doesn't have a limit
I embrace my second wind

Restoration is a blessing
I will not die prematurely
Overtaken and led by my emotions
and begin to choose poorly
I have plenty to offer
starting with the best of me
I anticipate the promises of EL
going after them aggressively

THE CONFLICT

Didn't want to get out of bed today
binding and rebuking depression
Praying for direction so my conscience can stay
Clear away from the guilt of getting
ahead of YAHUAH
*Can patience have her perfect work in the life
of a mountain mover?*
The walls are closing in
refuse to bow to evil doctrines
Walking by faith and not by sight
believing YAH is no option

Circumstances await my arrival
before I can offer Him my first fruits
Of praise and honor
mentalities of slaves and mourners dilute
The potency of the truth
sponsored by the physical sight
What is seen is temporary
for my salvation I fight

The world has a saying, "You can't win for losing."
all of these trials strengthen this warrior
I shall live and not die
fleeing from the face of the coroner
They say that home is where the heart is
in the mind of an artist…
I purpose to live life abundantly
before I'm dearly departed

Cornelius P. Thomas Jr.

My heart is in a wealthy place
a healthy space, dwelling safe
What I see in the natural paints a different picture
which calls for unfailing faith
Urged to grow and forced to go
despite the conflict that is seen
At times, we have to dig deeper
to bring up praise that will shift the scene

SPIRITUAL REHABILITATION

Standing guard at what seems to be
a standstill
Unsure of the present circumstances
and dilemmas
Feeling limited
due to the dysfunction within my surroundings
Suddenly, I am reminded
that creativity knows no boundaries
The determined part of me is grateful
for my present status and circumstances
In the dry place, dreaded feelings of despair
attempts to bombard a positive mental state
However, this is the place to embrace valuable lessons,
undergo construction and extensive training
Through trials and tribulations
one's beauty is defined
The seed that fought through the earth has been fighting
ever since the day that it was planted
The children of YAH are summoned
to turn obstacles into opportunities
I am thankful for the sacrifices of the previous
generation of faith walkers
The productive prayers that continue to linger
there are limitless opportunities for spiritual growth
My emotions stand
trapped by time
The Everlasting Spirit, by which I was baptized
acknowledges that YAHUAH can see
through the eyes of eternity

Cornelius P. Thomas Jr.

Today's lessons are essential in order to properly
handle tomorrow's promotions and blessings
In this life
accidents are few
…nothing is wasted on the journey
My character is subtly tested
as I am attacked by flaring tempers
We desperately need balance to truly operate
in the *Fruits of the Spirit*
Skills are learned
in the overlooked places of mediocrity
There is wisdom available to compensate
for the areas in which we lack
Experience is one of life's greatest teachers
the Ruach Ha'Qodesh is definitely the first
We must press on by faith
since there are no roles to rehearse
I'm glad that my salvation
doesn't depend on my feelings
In the belly of the beast
repenting for my rebellious mind state
Running from an assignment and ran
smack dab into true purpose
Shall I offer the fruit of my flesh for the
sin of my soul?
The flesh is only for a moment
spiritual rehabilitation is continual
I dare not limit the power of YAH
because my physical sight cannot comprehend
the Spirit's shifting
Isolation, situations, revelation, aggravation

transformation, manifestations…
In the heat of the day we're racing
waiting produces patience
Hoping for what I see not
eagerly anticipating another level
urged to make the most of this pit stop
The refining process
leads to the defining process
ELOHIYM is separating me
from dysfunction and unwanted things
The junk that holds no significant value
the blood of the Lamb never fails
Seems as if I am fighting a battle
that I will not win
…that is if I depend upon my own strength
Therefore, I surrender my all and submit
under the mighty *Hand of EL SHADDAI*
The flesh is only for a moment
spiritual rehabilitation is continual
The warfare is psychological
words rooted in emotions are kept at a minimal
capacity
Delegated authority means that all of heaven
is backing me
Calling those things that be not as though they were
pressing in with a bulldog tenacity

Cornelius P. Thomas Jr.

AT WAR WITH THE DEVIL'S KINGDOM

The Light of Christ is shining
the multitudes are blinded
We need healing for countless mindsets
this is war, not just words rhyming
Do we want integration or segregation?
Will we embrace unity or separation?
...embrace dignity or degradation?
I do this here for the Holy Nation
They say, "Make America great again."
while they're trying to decide our fate as men
I'm dwelling among the snakes that pretend
like they're friends, but cannot destroy my faith.. amends
Have been made
by the blood of the Lamb, we're sealed and kept
Part of the Body
but, the bloodline suffers from identity theft
Many of our forefathers fought and died
for rights of equality
Did they fail to repent for the disobedience and
exchange the royal covenant for idolatry?

Today, the lost generation is letting the previous
visions, dreams, dignity, and Biblical blueprint
slip through our fingers
Heavily sedated and overtaken
by the party scene
the demons behind the politics and the music
industry work hand in hand to promote
modern day slavery

Product of America

That's only to name a few
they strip the creative minds
of dignity and integrity
Originality is looked upon as lame
through the blinded eyes of the masses
However, modern technology
will never silence me
I have a mandate to speak the truth
no matter who gets tired of me
Always a cause to poetically protest
the battle started in the streets
I'm praying that these letters will ignite
Kingdom Builders worldwide to lay aside
petty quarrels and mediocrity
We have to commit and submit
to the leadership of the Holy Spirit
So that we can overthrow,
overcome and outlast all limitations
so that we may become true instruments of
change, open vessels that will operate in
miraculous signs and wonders
There is power, victory, and life
in the name of Jesus
True purpose is at hand
and she is calling for us to stand
We cannot continue to allow the media to shape
(what we think) is our culture
False leaders make vain contributions
feeding themselves like vultures
The media mocks and paint
a distorted picture of the church

Cornelius P. Thomas Jr.

They are controlled by the deceptive spirit
of the Anti-Christ
Demonic spirits are at war
with mighty destiny carriers
The Body of Christ
ELOHIYM is a Consuming Fire
Hypocritical mockers
soothsayers, religious demons, and witch doctors
Are strapped with artillery
but their weapons will not prosper
I continue to record my heart's melody
dying to self to keep faith and integrity
There are greater things ahead of me
call it a date with destiny
Executing through God-given lyrics of poetry
to deliver hope to the captives
Exposing the *Rock of my salvation*
His word is eternally established
Strength and liberty
is found within the Spirit of Truth
The Holy Spirit has formed a strategic alliance
with soldiers that have nothing to lose
I've been at the bottom
forsaken, battered, and bruised
In the face of strenuous persecution
urged to follow Heaven's rules
Before the world's foundation
I had a mandate to speak the truth
Every day is not a day of sunshine
however, every day is filled with hope
The blood of Christ is against

all the works of the devil
Those chosen to live a set apart life
represent an everlasting *Kingdom* that rules over all

Cornelius P. Thomas Jr.

BEGINNING OF SORROWS
Extended version

The spiritual war is unseen
it often hides behind politics
Hormone and chemical imbalances
I'm so tired of it
Far from positive
health is failing and many are sick
Health care, doctors, and pharmaceutical industries
are running scams, getting filthy rich

Everything has begun to switch
prescription drugs in the hands of thugs
People flee from the message of YAH
good hearts get drug through the mud
Modern technology and atomic energy
reveals the enemy
They destroy family relationships
pervert and suppress our true identities

Oil is big business
these countries are far from hurting
Gas prices fluctuate continually
many can't comprehend the evil lurking
The young nation continues to party
this is a fatherless generation
Self-destruction, extermination
lack of morals and education
Division and separation
among the closest of friends

Product of America

Deep within the hearts of men
is revealed the darkest sin
The earth rejects mankind
because they turned their backs on the Creator
Cursed are those who get caught without Him
laugh now and regret it later

Times of peril
guerrilla warfare is continuous
ELOHIYM is a burden bearer
some will still choose to carry the strenuous
Conditions and situations
trials and tribulations
People indirectly choose bondage
in the face of knowledge and liberation
Negative words are spoken to penetrate
but I'm protected by the Great…
I AM and the Lamb
who leads me for His name's sake

In the paths of righteousness
all men have gone astray
If one's heart is not hardened
one can receive Christ today
We're running out of time
don't take it for granted, the things of tomorrow
Without the stability of YAH it will get worse
The beginning of sorrows

Product of America

What is a product?

A thing or person that is the result of an action or process.

How is psychological warfare used?

It is used to induce confessions or reinforce attitudes and behaviors favorable to the originator's objectives. It is used to destroy the morale of enemies, through tactics that aim to depress troops' psychological states!

In closing, I could never cover this subject matter in depth in one setting. The rabbit hole of deception, subtle oppression, police brutality, wars declared in the name of religion, child and sex trafficking, identity theft, etc. runs deep. Therefore, I will momentarily say,
" …to be continued!"
REPENT! FOR THE KINGDOM OF YAH IS AT HAND!

www.ingramcontent.com/pod-product-compliance
Lightning Source LLC
Chambersburg PA
CBHW032057150426
43194CB00006B/556